AMERICA'S FAVORITE SYMBOLS

"THE STAR-SPANGLED BANNER"

THE U.S. NATIONAL ANTHEM

JINNOW KHALID

New York

Published in 2021 by The Rosen Publishing Group, Inc.
29 East 21st Street, New York, NY 10010

Portions of this work were originally authored by Maria Nelson and published as *The National Anthem*. All new material in this edition authored by Jinnow Khalid.

Editor: Elizabeth Krajnik
Book design: Reann Nye

Photo Credits: Cover, p.1 Tetra Images/Getty Images; Series Art sunwart/Shutterstock.com; p. 5 phloxii/Shutterstock.com; pp. 7, 11 Bettmann/Getty Images; p. 9 Courtesy of the Library of Congress; p 13 NICHOLAS KAMM/AFP/Getty Images; p. 15 https://commons.wikimedia.org/wiki/File:Fort_McHenry_flag.jpg; p. 17 Transcendental Graphics/Getty Images Sport/Getty Images; p. 19 Jayne Kamin-Oncea/Getty Images Sport/Getty Images; p. 21 GraphicaArtis/Archive Photos/Getty Images.

Library of Congress Cataloging-in-Publication Data

Names: Khalid, Jinnow, author.
Title: "The Star-Spangled Banner" : the U.S. national anthem / Jinnow Khalid.
Description: New York : PowerKids Press, [2021] | Series: America's favorite symbols | Includes index. |
Identifiers: LCCN 2019049455 | ISBN 9781725317314 (paperback) | ISBN 9781725317338 (library binding) | ISBN 9781725317321 (6 pack)
Subjects: LCSH: Baltimore, Battle of, Baltimore, Md., 1814–Juvenile literature. | Star-spangled banner (Song)–Juvenile literature. | United States–History–War of 1812–Flags–Juvenile literature. | Flags–United States–History–19th century–Juvenile literature. | Key, Francis Scott, 1779-1843–Juvenile literature.
Classification: LCC E356.B2 K44 2021 | DDC 784.7/1973-dc23
LC record available at https://lccn.loc.gov/2019049455

Manufactured in the United States of America

CPSIA Compliance Information: Batch #CSPK20. For Further Information contact Rosen Publishing, New York, New York at 1-800-237-9932.

CONTENTS

Symbol of America

"The Star-Spangled Banner" is the **national anthem** of the United States. The lyrics, or words of a song, remind us what it means to be an American. Since 1814, "The Star-Spangled Banner" has been a **symbol** of strength and **patriotism**.

The War of 1812

Problems remaining between the new United States and Great Britain after the **American Revolution** led to the countries going to war again on June 18, 1812. On August 24, 1814, British troops set fire to a number of buildings—including the White House—in Washington, D.C.

Freeing a Friend

Francis Scott Key, an American **lawyer**, boarded a British ship near Fort McHenry outside Baltimore, Maryland, to free a friend who'd been taken prisoner. The British agreed to free the other man—but not right away. Starting September 13, 1814, the British bombed Fort McHenry for 25 hours.

A
C

Winning the Battle

On the British ship, Key listened to and watched the British bomb Fort McHenry throughout the night. In the morning, he looked out and saw the American flag still waving above the fort. The Americans had won the battle!

"Defence of Fort M'Henry"

That morning, Key wrote a poem about what he'd seen. When he got back to Baltimore, he added more to the poem. Local newspapers later printed the poem as "Defence of Fort M'Henry." It was set to the tune of another song.

O say can you see ~~through~~ by the dawn's early light,
What so proudly we hail'd at the twilight's last gleaming,
Whose broad stripes & bright stars through the perilous fight
O'er the ramparts we watch'd, were so gallantly streaming?
And the rocket's red glare, the bomb bursting in air,
Gave proof through the night that our flag was still there,
O say does that star-spangled banner yet wave
O'er the land of the free & the home of the brave?

On the shore dimly seen through the mists of the deep,
Where the foe's haughty host in dread silence reposes,
What is that which the breeze, o'er the towering steep,
As it fitfully blows, half conceals, half discloses?
Now it catches the gleam of the morning's first beam,
In full glory reflected now shines in the stream,
'Tis the star-spangled banner — O long may it wave
O'er the land of the free & the home of the brave!

And where is that band who so vauntingly swore,
That the havoc of war & the battle's confusion
A home & a Country should leave us no more?
— ~~They have~~ Their blood has wash'd out their foul footsteps pollution.
No refuge could save the hireling & slave
From the terror of flight or the gloom of the grave,
And the star-spangled banner in triumph doth wave
O'er the land of the free & the home of the brave.

O thus be it ever when freemen shall stand
Between their lov'd home & the war's desolation!
Blest with vict'ry & peace may the heav'n rescued land
Praise the power that hath made & preserv'd us a nation!
Then conquer we must, when our cause it is just,
And this be our motto — "In God is our trust,"
And the star-spangled banner in triumph shall wave
O'er the land of the free & the home of the brave. —

Patriotic Song

By November 1812, Key's song was renamed "The Star-Spangled Banner." During and after the **American Civil War**, the song became even more popular because the flag was a symbol of unity. By the 1890s, the U.S. military played the song when the flag was raised and lowered.

FORT MCHENRY'S FLAG

Respecting the Soldiers

To show respect for the American soldiers fighting in World War I, a military band played "The Star-Spangled Banner" during the seventh inning of the first game of the 1918 World Series. Today, the song is played at all baseball games and many other events.

National Anthem

On March 3, 1931, President Herbert Hoover signed a law that made "The Star-Spangled Banner" the national anthem of the United States. Today, people sing the national anthem before sporting events and at government events. Often, people put their right hand over their heart to show respect.

LA
76
StateFarm
Spectrum
Security Benefit
Coca-Cola
OUR NATIONAL ANTHEM
UCLA Health
Spectrum
Security Benefit
OUR NATIONAL ANTHEM

The Flag Today

Today, you can see the same flag Francis Scott Key saw. It's been on **display** at the National Museum of American History since 1964. Over the years, people have tried to keep the flag in good shape. However, the flag is very **delicate**.

Timeline

September 13, 1814
British forces start bombing Fort McHenry.

September 14, 1814
American forces win the Battle of Baltimore. Francis Scott Key writes a poem, which is later set to music and printed as "Defence of Fort M'Henry."

1918
A military band plays "The Star-Spangled Banner" during the seventh inning of the first game of the World Series.

1931
President Herbert Hoover signs a law making "The Star-Spangled Banner" the national anthem of the United States.

1964
The star-spangled banner goes on display at the National Museum of American History.

GLOSSARY

American Civil War: A war fought from 1861 to 1865 between the North and the South in the United States over slavery and other issues.

American Revolution: A war that lasted from 1775 to 1783 in which the American colonists won independence from British rule.

delicate: Easily broken or damaged.

display: Put somewhere for people to see.

lawyer: A person whose job it is to guide and assist people in matters relating to the law.

national anthem: A song that praises a particular country and that is officially accepted as the country's song.

patriotism: Love that a person feels for their country.

symbol: Something that stands for something else.

INDEX

WEBSITES

Due to the changing nature of Internet links, PowerKids Press has developed an online list of websites related to the subject of this book. This site is updated regularly. Please use this link to access the list: www.powerkidslinks.com/afs/banner